Short, straight to the point desc
ing timeless truth in small dose:
after dinner.

Wayne Richards directs our thoughts to God
in an engaging and thoughtful way. Using the alphabet as a memory,
outlines 26 attributes of God, which should encourage and cheer us and our
family in the daily grind of life. This book will help us to look up instead of
inwardly to our own sinful heart and circumstances.

Carine Mackenzie
Children's author and Grandmother.

I found the benefit of this little gem to be summed up in the opening words of
the introduction: *'How much more healthy in mind and spirit would we be if we
focused more on God and less on ourselves?'* How true this is and how well Wayne
Richards helps us to consider God. The 26 devotionals each beginning with a
letter of the alphabet have beautiful scripture texts verifying the truth of what
has just been postulated. The great benefit of this devotional will be found if one
spends time meditating on its content rather than simply reading it through.

George I. MacAskill
Minister, Stornoway, Isle of Lewis

The word 'God' is just 3 tiny letters, yet the divine Person of God is, in every way,
endlessly uncontainable. You hold in your hand a little book, shaped by the 26
little letters of the alphabet. But what enormous, priceless treasures are contained
within these pages! In his clever, thoughtful, deliberate way, Wayne Richards
delivers true enormity with great economy. It's not catechism, nor creed, nor
confession, yet almost without realising it you will be drawn to consider the great
timeless truths of God's nature and character. It won't take you long to read this
cover-to-cover. But I'm sure you'll be drawn back again and again, to meditate
and marvel on Almighty God, portrayed so faithfully in this notebook for
eternity.

Colin Buchanan
Christian Children's Recording artist and author

Children's books winsomely teach reading by repetition. 'A' is for apple. 'B'
is for ball. What do all children of God need to learn? Answers to big questions — 'What is God really like?' Or, 'How will he receive me, a sinner?'
Finding reliable answers to eternal questions begins with knowing one's
spiritual ABC's. The Notebook for Eternity is a delightful, helpful primer
for all who long to know the one true, living God.

Ken Wingate
Author and Bible teacher

Scripture quotations are from The Holy Bible, English Standard Version Anglicised® (ESVUK ®), copyright © 2001 by Crossway, a publishing ministry of Good News Publishers. Used by permission.
All rights reserved.

Copyright © Wayne Richards 2018
paperback ISBN 978-1-52710-142-5
epub ISBN 978-1-5271-0198-2
mobi ISBN 978-1-5271-0199-9
First published in 2015
Reprinted in 2018
by
Christian Focus Publications Ltd
Geanies House, Fearn, Ross-shire
IV20 1TW, Scotland
www.christianfocus.com

Cover design by Daniel Van Straaten

Printed by Bell & Bain

Contents

Using this booklet

How much more healthy in mind and spirit would we be if we focused more on God and less on ourselves?

It is inborn to be obsessed with ourselves. That is called sin. Only God can change our bias. You cannot sin while contemplating God rightly. This daily devotional attempts to provide a tool to help remedy the imbalance. Use it to start or end the day, when saying grace or leading the family at mealtime. Read a section to someone ill or frail. Read it when you need to stop thinking about yourself and your own circumstances. It will be helpful when time is short or as a starter for more lengthy meditation, study and prayer.

No matter what our circumstances, we improve when we think beyond ourselves. When things went wrong for old Job he got a lot of poor advice as to why he was suffering so much and what he ought to do about it. But the cosmic agenda was never revealed to Job. However, when God came to him He provided Job with a simple but completely satisfying resolution. God says to Job, 'Look to ME! Contemplate ME!'

God is enough in every situation, good or bad. Considering God, who He is and what He has done and what He has promised to do, is all we ever need.

Of course there are more than twenty-six attributes of God. Build your own set (from the Bible)! If you were never catechised as a child each attribute of God attached to each letter of the English alphabet here becomes easy to learn and remember. They help us to place ourselves and our circumstances in right proportion to reality. They re-balance our perspective.

We forever try to make things simple but can often run the risk of becoming too simplistic. God is great and warrants great thoughts. God is more than love. Amazing grace has a context. Forgiveness costs. Eternity is real.

Meditating on God's nature will lead us to good thoughts, good feelings and good deeds. It will indeed lead us to a good place.

LMIGHTY

God is almighty. God is majestically infinite and powerful in every possible way. He is the ultimate sovereign reality. There is nothing that limits God nor does He contradict His own character. God is greater and accomplishes far beyond anything we can ever imagine. He is not just mighty, God is all mighty.

Mankind was created in the image of God. Yet, we have become perilously unlike God and corrupted in desperate need of redemption. Humankind now exhibits but a shadow of its original capacity. At our absolute best we remain finite and unreceptive to God. Deep down we know we can only find our meaning in Him.

'... I am God Almighty ...'   **GENESIS 17:1**

For the LORD your God is God of gods and Lord of lords, the great, the mighty, and the awesome God.

DEUTERONOMY 10:17a

Yours, O LORD, is the greatness and the power and the glory and the victory and the majesty, for all that is in the heavens and in the earth is yours. Yours is the kingdom, O LORD, and you are exalted as head above all. Both riches and honour come from you, and you rule over all. In your hand are power and might, and in your hand it is to make great and to give strength to all.   **1 CHRONICLES 29:11-12**

Our God is in the heavens; he does all that he pleases.

PSALM 115:3

B EAUTIFUL

God is beautiful. True beauty is more than what is materially pleasant to perceive in the cosmos, nature or design. Delightful splendour is also to be experienced in genuine meaning, music, words, mathematics, enterprise, relationships and holiness. The glory of God is so great a man cannot gaze upon it directly and live. Beauty is not simply a reflection of God, it finds its source and essence in God. The person, radiance, meaning, knowledge, decrees, purity and perfection of God is stunningly beautiful.

When this spiritual reality shines through to us we are readily attracted to it yet anxiously retreat from it, instinctively aware of our contrasting impoverishment.

Splendour and majesty are before him; strength and joy are in his place. **1 CHRONICLES 16:27**

Then the Almighty will be your gold and your precious silver. For then you will delight yourself in the Almighty and lift up your face to God. **JOB 22:25-26**

One thing have I asked of the LORD; that will I seek after: – that I may dwell in the house of the LORD all the days of my life, to gaze upon the beauty of the LORD and to enquire in his temple. **PSALM 27:4**

Splendour and majesty are before him; strength and beauty are in his sanctuary. **PSALM 96:6**

On the glorious splendour of your majesty, and on your wondrous works, I will meditate. **PSALM 145:5**

CREATOR

God is Creator. In the beginning God created everything. He created and sustains all that we can see as well as all that we cannot see. Nothing existed before God created it. Only God can create something from nothing. He established time, space, materiality and spirituality. God is not dependent on the laws of physics, chemistry or biology because He is the actual source of intelligence and reality, and is not bound within His own creation. The existence of moral goodness is merely a manifestation of God's own character.

Man is a creature. Our creativity reflects our Maker, but unlike God not all that we craft is good.

In the beginning, God created the heavens and the earth.

GENESIS 1:1

Great are the works of the LORD, studied by all who delight in them.

PSALM 111:2

Your hands have made and fashioned me; give me understanding that I may learn your commandments.

PSALM 119:73

All things were made through him, and without him was not any thing made that was made.

JOHN 1:3

'Worthy are you, our Lord and God, to receive glory and honour and power, for you created all things, and by your will they existed and were created.'

REVELATION 4:11

IVINE STANDARD

God is the divine standard. God's law reflects His character. Good things can be expressed both negatively and positively. In the Ten Commandments God forbids certain actions that He hates: disrespect and distrust towards Himself; disrespect for those in God-given authority (especially parents); disrespect for human life, for true marriage, for property or disrespect for truth (particularly concerning other people). In summary: do nothing which in any way dishonours God or your human neighbour who bears His image.

Jesus says the same thing positively: do everything that expresses the purpose of pleasing and exalting God and benefiting your neighbour (which is what 'love' for God and neighbour means).

And God spoke all these words, saying,
'I am the LORD your God, who brought you out of the land of Egypt, out of the house of slavery.

1. You shall have no other gods before me.
2. You shall not make for yourself a carved image ... You shall not bow down to them or serve them ...
3. You shall not take the name of the LORD your God in vain.
4. Remember the Sabbath day, to keep it holy ... For in six days the LORD made heaven and earth, the sea, and all that is in them, and rested on the seventh day. Therefore the LORD blessed the Sabbath day and made it holy.
5. Honour your father and your mother, that your days may be long in the land that the LORD your God is giving you.
6. You shall not murder.
7. You shall not commit adultery.
8. You shall not steal.
9. You shall not bear false witness against your neighbour.
10. You shall not covet your neighbour's house ... or anything that is your neighbour's.' **EXODUS 20:1-17**

... You shall love the Lord your God with all your heart and with all your soul and with all your mind and with all your strength ... You shall love your neighbour as yourself.

MARK 12:30-31a

E TERNAL

God is eternal. God has no beginning and is the real never-ending story. God is forever. He is from everlasting to everlasting. God unendingly existed before creation. He never began and will never cease. God has been and will always be there. God is not bound by time as we might comprehend it. God, the eternal One, is the absolute cause of time and sustains it by His eternal power. God pervades every moment of time with His eternity. God uses time to manifest His eternal attributes and accomplishments.

Everyone longs for eternity and eternal life after death. The all-powerful eternal God makes us that very offer.

'The LORD will reign forever and ever.' **EXODUS 15:18**

The eternal God is your dwelling place, and underneath are the everlasting arms. **DEUTERONOMY 33:27a**

Your throne is established from of old; you are from everlasting.

PSALM 93:2

For his invisible attributes, namely, his eternal power and divine nature, have been clearly perceived, ever since the creation of the world, in the things that have been made. So they are without excuse. **ROMANS 1:20**

'I am the Alpha and the Omega,' says the Lord God, 'who is and who was and who is to come, the Almighty.'

REVELATION 1:8

F AITHFUL

God is faithful. God can be fully trusted to be consistent and to do all that He promises to do. God is reliable and not fickle. He alone can be depended upon when everything looks lost. God knows what is best for us, and how and when to bring that about.

God calls for us to not trust in ourselves but to trust in Him alone. If we truly do that then God is faithful, even when we are not. Our faithfulness in doing right things will never reconcile us with God, but our faith in God will. God's faithfulness alone can secure the deliverance we all need.

Know therefore that the LORD your God is God, the faithful God who keeps covenant and steadfast love with those who love him and keep his commandments, to a thousand generations. **DEUTERONOMY 7:9**

Into your hand I commit my spirit; you have redeemed me, O LORD, faithful God. **PSALM 31:5**

From of old no one has heard or perceived by the ear, no eye has seen a God besides you, who acts for those who wait for him. **ISAIAH 64:4**

If we are faithless, he remains faithful—for he cannot deny himself. **2 TIMOTHY 2:13**

Let us hold fast the confession of our hope without wavering, for he who promised is faithful. **HEBREWS 10:23**

G RACIOUS

God is gracious. Grace is favour shown to those who deserve no favour at all. The message of the gospel is that a person can only get right with God for eternity solely and entirely by the grace of God, not by themselves. God graciously sent Christ, to suffer the consequences of our iniquity by dying on the cross and defeating death on our behalf – making it possible to bridge the chasm between God and the unworthy individual.

This priceless gift in grasping our need for forgiveness and believing that Jesus alone secured it, can only be received by personally relying upon the sacrifice of God the Son.

Yet you are he who took me from the womb; you made me trust you at my mother's breasts. **PSALM 22:9**

He who did not spare his own Son but gave him up for us all, how will he not also with him graciously give us all things? **ROMANS 8:32**

May the God of hope fill you with all joy and peace in believing, so that by the power of the Holy Spirit you may abound in hope. **ROMANS 15:13**

But he [the Lord] said to me, 'My grace is sufficient for you, for my power is made perfect in weakness.' Therefore I will boast all the more gladly of my weaknesses, so that the power of Christ may rest upon me. **2 CORINTHIANS 12:9**

But God, being rich in mercy, because of the great love with which he loved us, even when we were dead in our trespasses, made us alive together with Christ—by grace you have been saved—and raised us up with him and seated us with him in the heavenly places in Christ Jesus, so that in the coming ages he might show the immeasurable riches of his grace in kindness towards us in Christ Jesus. For by grace you have been saved through faith. And this is not your own doing; it is the gift of God, not a result of works, so that no one may boast. **EPHESIANS 2:4-9**

# H OLY

God is holy. Life is not about us, it is about God and His glory. We can only find our true identity in Him. God's glory is the inescapable weight of all His character and attributes. He is separate from all corruption and therefore we are separated from Him. God is a consuming fire, but in loving-kindness has not abandoned us. God spans an enormous gulf to allow us to approach Him safely. Through Christ alone, God has come near so we can be redeemed and, eventually, completely separated from our sin.

God's undefiled perfection should deeply humble us. The proper response to God's pure holiness is worship.

God reigns over the nations; God sits on his holy throne.

PSALM 47:8

Let them praise your great and awesome name! Holy is he!

PSALM 99:3

For thus says the One who is high and lifted up, who inhabits eternity, whose name is Holy: 'I dwell in the high and holy place, and also with him who is of a contrite and lowly spirit, to revive the spirit of the lowly, and to revive the heart of the contrite.'

ISAIAH 57:15

For he who is mighty has done great things for me, and holy is his name.

LUKE 1:49

Therefore let us be grateful for receiving a kingdom that cannot be shaken, and thus let us offer to God acceptable worship, with reverence and awe, for our God is a consuming fire.

HEBREWS 12:28-29

'Holy, holy, holy, is the Lord God Almighty, who was and is and is to come!'

REVELATION 4:8b

IRRESISTIBLE

God is irresistible. God never fails and is sovereign over everything, including effectively calling individuals to Himself. Our natural tendency is to avoid God but He alone can bring our resistance to an end. There is nothing a spiritually paralysed heart can do to make itself beat. We need a spiritual heart transplant before we can know spiritual reality – a new birth. Other than for the act of God the Father in deciding for us, God the Son atoning for us and God the Holy Spirit calling us – we are lost forever.

When the appetite is changed we willingly respond and taste and see that God is good.

Jesus answered him, 'Truly, truly, I say to you, unless one is born again he cannot see the kingdom of God.' **JOHN 3:3**

All that the Father gives me will come to me, and whoever comes to me I will never cast out. For I have come down from heaven, not to do my own will but the will of him who sent me. And this is the will of him who sent me, that I should lose nothing of all that he has given me, but raise it up on the last day. For this is the will of my Father, that everyone who looks on the Son and believes in him should have eternal life, and I will raise him up on the last day ... No one can come to me unless the Father who sent me draws him. And I will raise him up on the last day. It is written in the Prophets, 'And they will all be taught by God.' Everyone who has heard and learned from the Father comes to me ... And he said, 'This is why I told you that no one can come to me unless it is granted him by the Father.' **JOHN 6:37-40, 44-45, 65**

But he who enters by the door is the shepherd of the sheep. To him the gatekeeper opens. The sheep hear his voice, and he calls his own sheep by name and leads them out. When he has brought out all his own, he goes before them, and the sheep follow him, for they know his voice ... I am the good shepherd. I know my own and my own know me, just as the Father knows me and I know the Father; and I lay down my life for the sheep. And I have other sheep that are not of this fold. I must bring them also, and they will listen to my voice. So there will be one flock, one shepherd. **JOHN 10:2-4, 14-16**

J UST

God is just. Evil lives off good and strives to corrupt and tear it apart. God does not condone the smallest offence against His goodness. Everyone sins. We are the ones, not God, who unleashed the destructive power of hell into this once perfect world. Contaminating pride and self-reliance cannot survive in God's holy and righteous presence. God restrains wickedness from gaining full expression and will one day exile all that is not right and good, forever. Even in suffering God's delay is His merciful gift of time to allow reconciliation to Him.

God is all powerful and good. The Judge of all the earth will do right.

'Shall not the Judge of all the earth do what is just?'

GENESIS 18:25b

But the LORD sits enthroned forever; he has established his throne for justice, and he judges the world with righteousness; he judges the peoples with uprightness. PSALM 9:7-8

The works of his hands are faithful and just; all his precepts are trustworthy. PSALM 111:7

[There is a] righteousness of God through faith in Jesus Christ for all who believe. For there is no distinction: for all have sinned and fall short of the glory of God, and are justified by his grace as a gift, through the redemption that is in Christ Jesus ... It was to show his righteousness at the present time, so that he might be just and the justifier of the one who has faith in Jesus. ROMANS 3:22-24, 26

And I heard the altar saying, 'Yes, Lord God the Almighty, true and just are your judgements!' REVELATION 16:7

 NOWS ALL

God is knowledge. God is the unconditional source of all knowing and reality. God fully knows Himself and all things actual and possible in one simple and eternal act. Nothing is outside the scope of God's knowledge, which is comprehensive and exhaustive. God is light and in Him there is no darkness. God knows perfectly all that there is to know about the past, present and the future. God's knowledge is as extensive as His powerful control over everything. He knows the hidden essence of all things beyond the knowledge of mankind.

No creature is hidden from God. God penetrates to the very depths of the human heart.

Can you find out the deep things of God? Can you find out the limit of the Almighty? JOB 11:7

He who planted the ear, does he not hear? He who formed the eye, does he not see? He who disciplines the nations, does he not rebuke? He who teaches man knowledge—the LORD— knows the thoughts of man, that they are but a breath. PSALM 94:9-11

Great is our Lord, and abundant in power; his understanding is beyond measure. PSALM 147:5

Who has measured the Spirit of the LORD, or what man shows him his counsel? Whom did he consult, and who made him understand? Who taught him the path of justice, and taught him knowledge, and showed him the way of understanding? ... Have you not known? Have you not heard? The LORD is the everlasting God, the Creator of the ends of the earth. He does not faint or grow weary; his understanding is unsearchable. ISAIAH 40:13-14, 28

God ... knows everything. 1 JOHN 3:20b

LOVE

God is love. For God in His eternal goodness so loved the world He did an extraordinary thing; He gave His only Son for it. In loving-kindness God looked upon our fatal destiny and mercifully provided what we did not want, but desperately needed – a Redeemer. Only God's Son could absorb self-centred and dishonouring offences against a righteous God. Only God's love for us would allow such a sacrifice at Calvary. God would suffer unimaginably so that we might escape the consequences of sin and death. God tenderly extends forgiveness to the undeserving, if they place their trust in the costly offering of Jesus.

God loves the unlovely.

But the steadfast love of the LORD is from everlasting to everlasting on those who fear him, and his righteousness to children's children. **PSALM 103:17**

The LORD is my shepherd; I shall not want. He makes me lie down in green pastures. He leads me beside still waters. He restores my soul. He leads me in paths of righteousness for his name's sake. Even though I walk through the valley of the shadow of death, I will fear no evil, for you are with me; your rod and your staff, they comfort me. You prepare a table before me in the presence of my enemies; you anoint my head with oil; my cup overflows. Surely goodness and mercy shall follow me all the days of my life, and I shall dwell in the house of the LORD forever. **PSALM 23**

He brought me to the banqueting house, and his banner over me was love. **SONG OF SOLOMON 2:4**

That you, being rooted and grounded in love, may have strength to comprehend with all the saints what is the breadth and length and height and depth, and to know the love of Christ that surpasses knowledge. **EPHESIANS 3:17b-19a**

God is love. **1 JOHN 4:16b**

 ERCIFUL

God is merciful. God's great mercy flows from His goodness, love, compassion and pity. He is the Father of mercies and the God of all comfort. God is long-suffering, yet still shows us mercy when we are in misery or distress. God does not abandon us while we are on this earth. God comforts us in at least one or all of several ways; by removing the distress itself, by letting us see things from His better eternal perspective or He comes close and reveals more of Himself personally.

God's tender mercies should lead us from His sufficient grace for the moment, to His saving grace for eternity.

Remember your mercy, O LORD, and your steadfast love, for they have been from of old. Remember not the sins of my youth or my transgressions; according to your steadfast love remember me, for the sake of your goodness, O LORD!

PSALM 25:6-7

To us, O LORD, belongs open shame, to our kings, to our princes, and to our fathers, because we have sinned against you. To the Lord our God belong mercy and forgiveness, for we have rebelled against him and have not obeyed the voice of the LORD our God by walking in his laws, which he set before us by his servants the prophets.

DANIEL 9:8-10

The LORD is merciful and gracious, slow to anger and abounding in steadfast love.

PSALM 103:8

But when the goodness and loving kindness of God our Saviour appeared, he saved us, not because of works done by us in righteousness, but according to his own mercy, by the washing of regeneration and renewal of the Holy Spirit, whom he poured out on us richly through Jesus Christ our Saviour, so that being justified by his grace we might become heirs according to the hope of eternal life.

TITUS 3:4-7

N O OTHER

There is only one God. God is that of which nothing greater can be conceived. God is absolute and independent from everything else. He is self-contained, self-sustained, self-sufficient, self-authenticating, self-revealing and self-validating Deity. God transcends our highest thoughts. It is not that there is no other God like the God of the Bible; there is no other God at all. Jesus alone is the invisible God made visible. Every other promise for heaven says 'do this' but Christ says 'it is done'.

God is the first principle. None can usurp the supreme authority and reality of the One true God. There is no other name that is trustworthy.

Thus says the LORD, the King of Israel and his Redeemer, the LORD of hosts: 'I am the first and I am the last; besides me there is no god.   **ISAIAH 44:6**

... for I am God, and there is no other; I am God, and there is none like me.   **ISAIAH 46:9b**

Jesus said to him, 'I am the way, and the truth, and the life. No one comes to the Father except through me.'   **JOHN 14:6**

Until the appearing of our Lord Jesus Christ ... he who is the blessed and only Sovereign, the King of kings and Lord of lords, who alone has immortality, who dwells in unapproach-able light, whom no one has ever seen or can see. To him be honour and eternal dominion. Amen.   **1 TIMOTHY 6:14b-16**

To the King of ages, immortal, invisible, the only God, be honour and glory forever and ever. Amen.   **1 TIMOTHY 1:17**

And there is salvation in no one else, for there is no other name under heaven given among men by which we must be saved.   **ACTS 4:12**

OMNIPRESENT

God is omnipresent. God is present alongside time and space, absolutely everywhere. God is not confined by any place and is inescapable. God makes Himself felt in our heart and conscience. Everything is in God and He is in everything yet in different measures as He exhibits His presence in nature or through justice, or mercy or revealing His glory; either approving or disapproving – either close or far.

Those who seek God find Him not far away. For in Him we live and move and have our being. To draw near to Him is to become like Him; to move away from Him is to become unlike Him.

Where shall I go from your Spirit? Or where shall I flee from your presence? **PSALM 139:7**

The eyes of the LORD are in every place, keeping watch on the evil and the good. **PROVERBS 15:3**

'Am I a God at hand', declares the LORD, 'and not a God far away? Can a man hide himself in secret places so that I cannot see him?' declares the LORD. 'Do I not fill heaven and earth?' declares the LORD. **JEREMIAH 23:23-24**

Then will appear in heaven the sign of the Son of Man, and then all the tribes of the earth will mourn, and they will see the Son of Man coming on the clouds of heaven with power and great glory. **MATTHEW 24:30**

... God ... is actually not far from each one of us, for 'In him we live and move and have our being' ... **ACTS 17:27b-28a**

PEACE

God is the God of peace. Peace from God defies understanding. It prevails in the darkest of times. Ultimately, God makes everything work towards good, particularly for the good of those who love Him. The gospel is the message of deliverance from conflict, anxiety, unhappiness, evil, ourselves and death. True peace is only available from God. Christ, the Prince of Peace, represents the fullness of salvation: personal peace, completeness, wholeness, fullness and the prosperity of eternity. The God of peace gives true and lasting joy.

Augustine (A.D. 354-370) confessed to God, 'You made us for yourself, and our heart is restless, until it finds its rest in you.'

Surely his salvation is near to those who fear him, that glory may dwell in our land. Steadfast love and faithfulness meet; righteousness and peace kiss each other. **PSALM 85:9-10**

For to us a child is born, to us a son is given; and the government shall be upon his shoulder, and his name shall be called Wonderful Counsellor, Mighty God, Everlasting Father, Prince of Peace. **ISAIAH 9:6**

You keep him in perfect peace whose mind is stayed on you, because he trusts in you. **ISAIAH 26:3**

Peace I leave with you; my peace I give to you. Not as the world gives do I give to you. Let not your hearts be troubled, neither let them be afraid. **JOHN 14:27**

Rejoice in the Lord always; again I will say, Rejoice. Let your reasonableness be known to everyone. The Lord is at hand; do not be anxious about anything, but in everything by prayer and supplication with thanksgiving let your requests be made known to God. And the peace of God, which surpasses all understanding, will guard your hearts and your minds in Christ Jesus. **PHILIPPIANS 4:4-7**

UICK TO BLESS

God is slow to anger. God Himself is the ultimate supreme good for His creatures. God freely pours out His blessing upon creation. God did not create the world out of need but out of goodness. We cannot change, increase or decrease Him in any way. God's blessings are wonderfully seen in His many provisions, mercy and grace – unmerited favour to rebels. Humble expression of appreciation in prayer is an appropriate response for God's many blessings.

Because God is personal we have the prospect of approaching and speaking with Him. We have the privilege to praise, thank, confess and ask God for help – for others, and ourselves.

In every place where I cause my name to be remembered I will come to you and bless you. **EXODUS 20:24b**

The LORD bless you and keep you; the LORD make his face to shine upon you and be gracious to you; the LORD lift up his countenance upon you and give you peace.
NUMBERS 6:24-26

Blessed are all who take refuge in him. **PSALM 2:12c**

Blessed is the one whose transgression is forgiven, whose sin is covered. **PSALM 32:1**

And he said to them, 'When you pray, say: "Father, hallowed be your name. Your kingdom come. Give us each day our daily bread, and forgive us our sins, for we ourselves forgive everyone who is indebted to us. And lead us not into temptation."'
LUKE 11:2-4

And we know that for those who love God all things work together for good, for those who are called according to his purpose. **ROMANS 8:28**

R EDEEMER

God is redeemer. There is a difference between innocence and guilt; safe and unsafe. We cannot redeem ourselves. Initially, redemption is a transaction within the Holy Trinity of God. The Son offers Himself to the Father as our substitute. God both judges and is judged. The Spirit applies this divine exchange to reconcile us to God. Christ restores God's honour and His victory becomes our victory over sin and death. Because Jesus now lives, those who trust Him rather than themselves, shall also live.

A just God must uphold what is right. Yet, a loving God makes available at great cost that which we could never achieve for ourselves.

For I know that my Redeemer lives, and at the last he will stand upon the earth. And after my skin has been thus destroyed, yet in my flesh I shall see God.   **JOB 19:25-26**

... And you shall know that I, the LORD, am your Saviour and your Redeemer, the Mighty One of Jacob.   **ISAIAH 60:16b**

This Jesus, delivered up according to the definite plan and foreknowledge of God, you crucified and killed by the hands of lawless men. God raised him up, loosing the pangs of death, because it was not possible for him to be held by it.

ACTS 2:23-24

But we preach Christ crucified, a stumbling block to Jews and folly to Gentiles, but to those who are called, both Jews and Greeks, Christ the power of God and the wisdom of God.

1 CORINTHIANS 1:23-24

Waiting for our blessed hope, the appearing of the glory of our great God and Saviour Jesus Christ.   **TITUS 2:13**

S PEAKS

God has spoken. The incomprehensible One, makes Himself known. God speaks in nature but more fully in Scripture; by ordinary and extraordinary means. God not only created and sustains an entire universe, He created and sustains one book – the Bible. The Bible is special revelation of God and redemption. God is wise and gracious enough to make Himself known and accessible to anyone. Through the Living Word – Christ Jesus, we hear Him calling us personally to participate in the historical work of grace by His gift of faith.

The Bible is absolutely necessary, clearly understandable, perfectly enough and also the final true authoritative word concerning God and mankind.

God is not man, that he should lie, or a son of man, that he should change his mind. Has he said, and will he not do it? Or has he spoken, and will he not fulfil it? **NUMBERS 23:19**

This God—his way is perfect; the word of the LORD proves true. **2 SAMUEL 22:31a**

But his delight is in the law of the Lord, and on his law he meditates day and night **PSALM 1:2**

But he answered, 'It is written, "Man shall not live by bread alone, but by every word that comes from the mouth of God."' **MATTHEW 4:4**

Long ago, at many times and in many ways, God spoke to our fathers by the prophets, but in these last days he has spoken to us by his Son, whom he appointed the heir of all things, through whom also he created the world. **HEBREWS 1:1-3a**

For the word of God is living and active, sharper than any two-edged sword, piercing to the division of soul and of spirit, of joints and of marrow, and discerning the thoughts and intentions of the heart. **HEBREWS 4:12**

T RIUNE

God is three in One while there remains only One God. Plurality within the Godhead is God's special mark of distinction. God is the sole, self-existent Deity in undivided eternal community of three distinct but not separate persons mutually indwelling each other – God the Father, God the Son and God the Holy Spirit – identical in substance, equal in power and glory, sharing all things. Three in One may be difficult to understand, yet it is what Scripture teaches concerning God. Idolatry contemplates God other than as One, in three persons.

The Holy Spirit enables infiltration of the mystery of that divine fellowship which Christians experience as the Trinity.

... in the name of the Father and of the Son and of the Holy Spirit.   **MATTHEW 28:19b**

... the Spirit descending on him like a dove. And a voice came from heaven, 'You are my beloved Son; with you I am well pleased.'   **MARK 1:10b-11**

'But when the Helper comes, whom I will send to you from the Father, the Spirit of truth, who proceeds from the Father, he will bear witness about me.'   **JOHN 15:26**

The grace of the Lord Jesus Christ and the love of God and the fellowship of the Holy Spirit be with you all.
                                    2 CORINTHIANS 13:14

His divine power has granted to us all things that pertain to life and godliness, through the knowledge of him who called us to his own glory and excellence, by which he has granted to us his precious and very great promises, so that through them you may become partakers of the divine nature, having escaped from the corruption that is in the world because of sinful desire.   **2 PETER 1:3-4**

UNCHANGING

God is unchanging. God is complete. It is impossible for God to change. He cannot change for the worse because He is holy, and He cannot change for the better because He is already perfect. God is unchangeable and incorruptible in His essence and being. What He says, He will do, and He always completes what He has begun. God is the sole cause of all that changes and can enter into an infinite number of relations with His creatures while remaining unchanged in His nature.

The difference between the Creator and the creature, hinges on the vast contrast between being and becoming. God is our permanent Rock.

Trust in the LORD forever, for the LORD GOD is an everlasting rock. **ISAIAH 26:4**

For I the LORD do not change; therefore you, O children of Jacob, are not consumed. **MALACHI 3:6**

For the gifts and the calling of God are irrevocable. **ROMANS 11:29**

So when God desired to show more convincingly to the heirs of the promise the unchangeable character of his purpose, he guaranteed it with an oath, so that by two unchangeable things, in which it is impossible for God to lie, we who have fled for refuge might have strong encouragement to hold fast to the hope set before us. We have this as a sure and steadfast anchor of the soul. **HEBREWS 6:17-19a**

Jesus Christ is the same yesterday and today and forever. **HEBREWS 13:8**

Every good gift and every perfect gift is from above, coming down from the Father of lights with whom there is no variation or shadow due to change. **JAMES 1:17**

Victorious

God is victorious. Evil forces pitch themselves against God but God never loses. God can never be outmanoeuvred, taken by surprise, or caught at a disadvantage. God knows no crisis. The atoning death and resurrection of Jesus was no accident or nice life example – it was a sacrificial plan that achieved a holy outcome. Before any emergency arises God in His providence has already made a more than adequate and perfectly timed provision to meet it, for those who place their dependence upon Him.

On Judgement Day everything wrong will be put right and every tear wiped away. All that is good will never be contaminated again.

And the ransomed of the LORD shall return and come to Zion with singing; everlasting joy shall be upon their heads; they shall obtain gladness and joy, and sorrow and sighing shall flee away.   **ISAIAH 35:10**

For he must reign until he has put all his enemies under his feet.   **1 CORINTHIANS 15:25**

... for it is written, 'As I live, says the Lord, every knee shall bow to me, and every tongue shall confess to God.'   **ROMANS 14:11**

... so that at the name of Jesus every knee should bow, in heaven and on earth and under the earth, and every tongue confess that Jesus Christ is Lord, to the glory of God the Father.   **PHILIPPIANS 2:10-11**

And I heard a loud voice from the throne saying, 'Behold, the dwelling place of God is with man. He will dwell with them, and they will be his people, and God himself will be with them as their God. He will wipe away every tear from their eyes, and death shall be no more, neither shall there be mourning, nor crying, nor pain any more, for the former things have passed away.'   **REVELATION 21:3-4**

WISE

God is wise. God is infallible and unchanging in His wisdom. Wisdom is seeing and choosing the best and highest goal while applying the surest means of achieving it. Therefore, perfect wisdom is found only in God. God is never indecisive or makes a wrong decision. God always knows best. In Scripture the wisdom of God is personalised and described as the Word – Jesus.

Surprisingly, God chiefly displays His many-faceted and manifold wisdom within the redeemed community of God – the Church. It is there we witness the wisdom of His grace, love, mercy, kindness, long-suffering and His gentleness displayed to the sinful sons and daughters of Adam.

O LORD, how manifold are your works! In wisdom have you made them all. **PSALM 104:24a**

It is he who made the earth by his power, who established the world by his wisdom, and by his understanding stretched out the heavens. **JEREMIAH 10:12**

And coming to his home town he taught them in their synagogue, so that they were astonished, and said, 'Where did this man get this wisdom and these mighty works?' **MATTHEW 13:54**

In the beginning was the Word, and the Word was with God, and the Word was God. He was in the beginning with God ... In him was life, and the life was the light of men. The light shines in the darkness, and the darkness has not overcome it. **JOHN 1:1-2, 4-5**

Oh, the depth of the riches and wisdom and knowledge of God! How unsearchable are his judgements and how inscrutable his ways! **ROMANS 11:33**

 ROSS

The cross of Christ is the pivot of all history. God has a holy intolerance of evil and sin. Instead of inflicting upon us the judgement we deserved, Christ endured it in our place. Christ dying on the cross is the event in which God makes known His holiness and His love simultaneously in one event where the penalties of uncompromising righteousness combine with transcendent love. The biblical gospel of atonement is about God satisfying His righteous character by substituting Himself for us.

That someone else pays and that this be God Himself causes some to proudly prefer to perish rather than humbly repent before this holy God.

And when they came to the place that is called The Skull, there they crucified him, and the criminals, one on his right and one on his left … The women who had come with him from Galilee followed and saw the tomb and how his body was laid … He is not here, but has risen. Remember how he told you, while he was still in Galilee, that the Son of Man must be delivered into the hands of sinful men and be crucified and on the third day rise. **LUKE 23:33, 55; 24:6-7**

For in him all the fullness of God was pleased to dwell, and through him to reconcile to himself all things, whether on earth or in heaven, making peace by the blood of his cross. **COLOSSIANS 1:19-20**

… God made alive together with him, having forgiven us all our trespasses, by cancelling the record of debt that stood against us with its legal demands. This he set aside, nailing it to the cross. He disarmed the rulers and authorities and put them to open shame, by triumphing over them in him. **COLOSSIANS 2:13b-15**

Looking to Jesus, the founder and perfecter of our faith, who for the joy that was set before him endured the cross, despising the shame, and is seated at the right hand of the throne of God. **HEBREWS 12:2**

Humble yourselves, therefore, under the mighty hand of God so that at the proper time he may exalt you. **1 PETER 5:6**

AHWEH

God is Yahweh. God made Himself known to ancient Israel as יהוה (YHWH) and to the Christian Church as Father. The Old and New Testament Scriptures reveal God to us as Yahweh – the LORD. Jesus is LORD. Yahweh is the covenant God of promise, the faithful and powerful One who delivers His people – the great 'I AM'. Christ introduced the new personal name of 'Father', indicating God's special relationship with His people.

'Father' is the supreme revelation of God, and since the Father is made known to us by Jesus through the Spirit, the full revelation of God's name is Trinitarian: Father, Son and Holy Spirit.

Then Moses said to God, 'If I come to the people of Israel and say to them, "The God of your fathers has sent me to you", and they ask me, "What is his name?" what shall I say to them?' God said to Moses, 'I AM WHO I AM.' And he said, 'Say this to the people of Israel, "I AM has sent me to you."' God also said to Moses, 'Say this to the people of Israel, "The LORD, the God of your fathers, the God of Abraham, the God of Isaac, and the God of Jacob, has sent me to you." This is my name for ever, and thus I am to be remembered throughout all generations. **EXODUS 3:13-15**

Holy and awesome is his name! **PSALM 111:9b**

And I will vindicate the holiness of my great name, which has been profaned among the nations, and which you have profaned among them. And the nations will know that I am the LORD, declares the Lord GOD, when through you I vindicate my holiness before their eyes. **EZEKIEL 36:23**

And because you are sons, God has sent the Spirit of his Son into our hearts, crying, 'Abba! Father!' **GALATIANS 4:6**

Z EALOUS

God is zealous for His eternal purpose. The world is governed by the decrees of God alone. He is determined to see His declarations fulfilled. God's providence directs nature and history and succeeds because of His steadfast consistency to Himself and His Word. The impulse that drives everything God is and does is His own glory.

The chief end of man is to glorify God and to enjoy Him forever. Likewise the chief end of God is to glorify and to enjoy Himself forever. This is the goal of God's covenant love toward us. God is zealous for His cause and invites us to participate in His joy.

Delight yourself in the LORD, and he will give you the desires of your heart. **PSALM 37:4**

Of the increase of his government and of peace there will be no end, on the throne of David and over his kingdom, to establish it and to uphold it with justice and with righteousness from this time forth and for evermore. The zeal of the LORD of hosts will do this. **ISAIAH 9:7**

For the LORD of hosts has purposed, and who will annul it? His hand is stretched out, and who will turn it back? **ISAIAH 14:27**

My counsel shall stand, and I will accomplish all my purpose. **ISAIAH 46:10b**

The LORD will fulfil his purpose for me; your steadfast love, O LORD, endures for ever. **PSALM 138:8a**

This was according to the eternal purpose that he has realized in Christ Jesus our Lord. **EPHESIANS 3:11**

I cannot rightly know myself if I do not know God

Life is not about me, it is about God – His purpose and His glory.

I know who made the world, heaven and earth, and the entire universe. I know why He created me and what my destiny is.

My chief purpose is to glorify God and fully enjoy Him forever. My destiny is eternal joy. God has planted in my human consciousness the great idea that true life can be found only in fellowship with Him. God will be the source of endless delight because He has made known to me the riches of His glory.

I am no longer in an adversarial relationship toward God. Christ by His cross achieved a victory over sin and death for me, bringing immortality and light. The wrath of God no longer weighs on me. Everyone who believes in Him has eternal life and will never die.

Christ is the true prophet, priest and king; the true servant of the LORD, the true atonement, the true sacrifice, and His body of believers are the true offspring of Abraham; the true Israel and the true people of God.

My true identity is found in God and can only continue in Him. I am redeemed by God from myself and all evil. I am an adopted child of the living God, a member of His family and a partaker in the divine nature.

The heart cannot imagine what God has prepared for those who love Him.

I am not a body with a soul –
I am a soul with a body

My communion with Christ and my possession of real life has begun now and will be completed with Him in eternity. My spirit will be made perfect.

Death is the big interruption – the final enemy, but Jesus has removed its sting. My soul will be in the presence of God immediately after I die. All causes of grief and sorrow will be removed. Pain, illness, tiring work, struggle, poverty, dishonour and sadness will all be gone. I will be given every good pleasure which I have neither earned nor deserve. Joy will be so great that none greater is possible. My treasure is in heaven. I will meet again those dearly loved fellow believers, family and friends whom I have missed.

I will be on the winning side of God's limitless power and love – His infinite, eternal and unchangeable beauty, holiness and wisdom. Together with an uncountable number I will be taken up into the same heaven, be at home with the same Lord, enjoy the same rest and find joy in the same service of God. Such service coinciding with resting and enjoying.

The Son of God will return and usher in a new heaven and a new earth. He will judge the earth but I will be safe in Him. For the main issue in the final judgement is that of faith or unbelief. Faith in Christ is the work of God. Together with all those who believe I will appear before the judgement seat of Christ, however I will not enter judgement like those who do not believe. They shall come under condemnation to their eternal ruin. The final judgement will be a global and public vindication of Christ's rule. Every culture and society will be exposed as not being superior to a life lived in the true gospel of God. My soul will be given a new body like Christ's and I will be raised incorruptible and glorious.

As a simple vessel of mercy, I am blessed by the Father to inherit a kingdom prepared for me from the foundation of the world.

I can be confident

But how can a Christian be so confident and have such assurance in being able to make these statements? It comes down to the view I hold of Christ. He either is who He claims to be or He is not. If He is, He can achieve all that He promises. God being sovereign over everything causes there to be meaning in everything – ultimately good meaning. If God is truly sovereign over absolutely everything, then He is also sovereign over my salvation and so I repent and cease from thinking and acting as if I am the sovereign one.

The Holy Spirit of God bears witness with the spirit of each individual Christian that they are forgiven and their name is written in the Lamb's book of life. When someone believes in God's Word – they do not believe God because they have subjected God to tests which He manages to pass! God gets through regardless. God's Word is the judge of what is valid and sound reasoning.

God writes Himself on my heart, confirming the truth and reliability of Scripture – and though I am totally depraved, God unconditionally saves me at His good pleasure by the work of Christ on the cross so that I cannot resist His offer of life, and He will therefore ensure that I persevere safely to the very end. It no longer depends on me.

This same conviction is readily and freely available 'if you confess with your mouth that Jesus is Lord and believe in your heart that God raised him from the dead, you will be saved' (Romans 10:9).

Now as I look into the mirror of God's revelation, I only see his image; soon I will see Him face to face and know as I am known. Contemplation, understanding and enjoyment of God make up the essence of my future blessedness. The redeemed shall see God ... in a way that far outstrips all current revelation. And so I will know Him ... with a knowledge that has its image and likeness in God's knowledge – directly, immediately, unambiguously and purely. Then I will receive and possess everything I expected in hope. So contemplating and possessing God I shall enjoy Him and be blessed in his fellowship: blessed in soul and body, in heart, intellect and will ... The difference between night and day will be suspended. Time will be charged with the eternity of God. Space will be full of his presence. Eternal becoming wedded to immutable being. Even the contrast between heaven and earth will be gone.

Herman Bavinck, Reformed Dogmatics Vol 4, p722 & 729. Baker Academic (paraphrased).

Index

Christian Focus Publications

Our mission statement –

STAYING FAITHFUL

In dependence upon God we seek to impact the world through literature faithful to His infallible Word, the Bible. Our aim is to ensure that the Lord Jesus Christ is presented as the only hope to obtain forgiveness of sin, live a useful life and look forward to heaven with Him.

Our books are published in four imprints:

CHRISTIAN FOCUS

Popular works including biographies, commentaries, basic doctrine and Christian living.

CHRISTIAN HERITAGE

Books representing some of the best material from the rich heritage of the church.

MENTOR

Books written at a level suitable for Bible College and seminary students, pastors, and other serious readers. The imprint includes commentaries, doctrinal studies, examination of current issues and church history.

CF4·K

Children's books for quality Bible teaching and for all age groups: Sunday school curriculum, puzzle and activity books; personal and family devotional titles, biographies and inspirational stories – because you are never too young to know Jesus!

Christian Focus Publications Ltd,
Geanies House, Fearn, Ross-shire,
IV20 1TW, Scotland, United Kingdom.
www.christianfocus.com
blog.christianfocus.com